Dear friend,

It is my sincere hope that your child enjoys this compilation of the titles of His Holiness Bahá'u'lláh, and that it will lead to further insights on His station, as they reflect on the significance of each title bestowed upon Him.

Picture books are a great way to talk about a topic to children, as they provide a visual tool to process information. The words, accompanied by uplifting illustrations, often trigger questions and observations of their inquisitive minds and pure hearts. This in turn provides many opportunities to learn, through their personal reflection and your loving guidance.

The titles chosen here are only a few examples and many more can be found within the Holy Writings of the Bahá'í Faith. The choice of titles, the order, as well as the illustrations that accompany them, should by no means limit your conversation and reflection about the implications of Bahá'u'll'áh's titles and His station, nor should the choices here be seen as suggestions to regard them as being of more significance than others.

It is my humble hope that this book provides a tool to contribute to uplifting conversations in homes, as well as to your child's ever growing understanding on the Personage of Bahá'u'lláh as they continue to strengthen their ability to "Meditate profoundly, that the secret of things unseen may be revealed unto you [...]." (Bahá'u'lláh, The Kitáb-i-'Iqán, p.9).

Much love and prayers coming your way, wherever you may be.

Helen

*To the pioneers and Knights of Baháu'lláh,
who took His Name to every corner of the world.* H.F.

To Farzam, Luca & Zayden, my constant source of inspiration. L.K.S.

Fresh Breeze Creations

All rights reserved.

No parts of this publication may be reproduced, stored in a retrieval system, or transmitted, in any form or by any means, without prior written permission of the author.

Text Copyright: Helen Flynn   Fresh.Breeze.Creations@gmail.com   fresh_breeze_creations

Illustration Copyright: Louisa Kwan Shabani   Louisakshabani@gmail.com   lou_illustrates

The Glory of God

Compilation by Helen Flynn

Illustrations by Louisa Kwan Shabani

the Sun of Wisdom.

I am
the Most Great Name.

I am the Refuge for the fearful.

I AM THE MOST MIGHTY INSTRUMENT.

I am the Day Star of the Universe.

I am the royal Falcon on the arm of the Almighty.

I am Bahá'u'lláh, the Glory of God.

Who is Bahá'u'lláh?

Bahá'u'lláh is the Supreme Manifestation of God, foretold by His Herald the Báb. He is the Prophet Founder of the youngest world religion, namely the Bahá'í Faith. Bahá'ís believe Bahá'u'lláh to be the latest in a chain of Manifestations, sent by God from time to time, to assist humanity in its natural progression by re-establishing its covenant with God and calling humanity to its inherent nobility.

Bahá'u'lláh Himself was born in the province of Núr in Iran on the 12th November 1817, to a noble household. His family was among the wealthy in Persia of that time and was well respected. Declining to take on a high position in the court of the Sháh as His father's successor, Bahá'u'lláh as a young man chose to dedicate His time to the poor and needy and thus became known as the Father of the Poor. Even in His earliest childhood He showed little regard for the material wealth many aspire to and rather focused on spiritual matters.

Bahá'u'lláh sacrificed all He had as soon as He heard the call of the Báb through receiving some of His Writings. From that day He lived to teach the Faith of the Báb, despite arousing the animosity and strong opposition from the Persian government and clergy. His growing fame led to four months of imprisonment in the Siyah-Chál, also known as the Black Pit. What followed was the banishment from His native land, marking the beginning of forty years of exile, further imprisonment and persecution for Him and His family. This however, Bahá'u'lláh accepted with a cheerful heart.

Bahá'u'lláh received the call from God to arise as the Promised One of mankind and to lead the people aright whilst still imprisoned in 1852. He waited until 1863 to declare His mission publically in the Garden of Ridván.

During the forty years of His ministry, Bahá'u'lláh brought new social and spiritual teachings to address the needs of our time. Among His teachings are the equality of men and women, the need for universal education, that all of the world's religions are from God, that humanity is one and that it is time to work towards the establishment of world unity.

For further reading on the personage of Bahá'u'lláh, please visit the following websites https://www.bahaullah.org/ , http://www.bahai.org/bahaullah/ or contact your local Bahá'í community.

Hi you!

I hope this book has brought you much joy and helped you think about some of the titles of Bahá'u'lláh.

Now it is your turn.

Be a seeker of knowledge and find another title of Bahá'u'lláh. Many more can be found in the Holy Writings. You can ask someone you love to help you with this task and find the right book for you. Once you have found a title, reflect about it and talk about what it means to you. Then draw a picture of it, remembering not to draw Bahá'u'lláh Himself of course.

I would love to see what your heart is inspired to do. If you like and are allowed, please send me a picture of your drawing. You can email it to fresh.breeze.creations@gmail.com

I hope this brings as much joy to you as it has to me and Louisa.

Much love and prayers coming to you, wherever you may be.

Helen

References

I am the Sun of Wisdom

Bahá'u'lláh. (1988). Tablets of Bahá'u'lláh Revealed after the Kitáb-i-Aqdas. (S. Effendi and other committees and individuals, Trans.). Haifa: Bahá'í World Centre. (Original work published 1873-1892)

I am the Ocean of Knowledge

Bahá'u'lláh. (1988). Tablets of Bahá'u'lláh Revealed after the Kitáb-i-Aqdas. (S. Effendi and other committees and individuals, Trans.). Haifa: Bahá'í World Centre. (Original work published 1873-1892)

I am the guiding the Light that illumineth the way

Bahá'u'lláh. (1988). Tablets of Bahá'u'lláh Revealed after the Kitáb-i-Aqdas. (S. Effendi and other committees and individuals, Trans.). Haifa: Bahá'í World Centre. (Original work published 1873-1892)

I am the Beauty of God amongst you

Bahá'u'lláh. (2002). Summons of the Lord of Hosts.(S. Effendi and other committees and individuals, Trans.) Bahá'í World Centre. (Original work published 1868)

I am the Hidden Treasure

Bahá'u'lláh. (1988.) Tablets of Bahá'u'lláh revealed after the Kitáb-i-Aqdas. (S. Effendi and other committees and individuals, Trans.).US Bahá'i Publishing Trust. (Original work published 1978)

I am the Most Great Name

Effendi, S. (2000). God Passes By. (Rev. Ed.) Wilmette: US Bahá'í Pub Publishing Trust.

I am the Refuge for the Fearful

Bahá'u'lláh. (1987). Prayers and Meditations by Bahá'u'lláh. (S. Effendi, Trans.). US Bahá'í Publishing Trust. (Original work published 1863-1892)

I am the Pen of Revelation

Bahá'u'lláh. (1990). Gleanings from the writings of Bahá'u'lláh. S. Effendi, Trans.) Wilmette:US Bahá'í Publishing Trust. (Original work published 1863-1892)

I am the Most Mighty Instrument

Bahá'u'lláh. (2002). The Summons of the Lord of Hosts. (S. Effendi and other committees and individuals, Trans.). Haifa: Bahá'í World Centre. (Original work published 1868)

I am the Day Star of the Universe

Effendi, S. (2000). God Passes By (Rev.ed.) Wilmette:US Bahá'í Publishing Trust.

I am the royal Falcon on the arm of the Almighty

Bahá'u'lláh. (1988). Tablets of Bahá'u'lláh Revealed after the Kitáb-i-Aqdas. (S. Effendi and other committees and individuals, Trans.). Haifa: Bahá'í World Centre. (Original work published 1873-1892)

I am the Pre-Existent Root

Effendi, S. (2000). God Passes By. (Rev. Ed.). Wilmette: US Bahá'í Publishing Trust.

www.ingramcontent.com/pod-product-compliance
Lightning Source LLC
Chambersburg PA
CBHW041431010526
44107CB00046B/1574